ICONIC BRITAIN

Published by VisitBritain Publishing, Thames Tower, Blacks Road, London W6 9EL

First published 2007

© British Tourist Authority (trading as VisitBritain) 2007

ISBN
978 0 7095 8396 7
Product code: IMAGES04

A CIP catalogue record for this book is available from the British Library.

All the photographs in *Iconic Britain* were selected from VisitBritain's official online image library, Britain on View.

Editorial and design by Indigo 3 Publishing for VisitBritain Publishing.
Reprographics by CTT Limited.
Printed and bound in Dubai by Oriental Press.

Front cover: Stonehenge by Britain on View

ICONIC BRITAIN

ICONIC  BRITAIN

Iconic Britain provides a fascinating snapshot of the cosmopolitan character and idiosyncratic nature of a historic nation embracing the future, a nation with monuments and customs known the world over – from Stonehenge and the Angel of the North to bagpipes, cream teas and fish and chips.

Iconic Britain showcases many of Britain's best-loved castles, cathedrals and monuments – Caernarfon Castle, York Minster, the Eden Project – but also provides an insight into its many local characteristics, such as morris dancing, punting and the Highland Games, painting a picture of a nation that is as diverse as it is colourful.

Taken from Britain on View, VisitBritain's own image library,
the stunning selection of photographs in this book gives
a unique insight into the life of a nation, as well as its great
sights. *Iconic Britain* also includes a useful gazetteer of visitor
information and contact details for many of the places and
destinations featured.

The iron work was cast and put together in a very masterly manner... and the whole was completed in the year 1779. The design was original and very bold, and was, as far as the iron work goes, well executed.

THOMAS TELFORD

13

21

*There is no trouble so great
or grave that cannot be diminished
by a nice cup of tea.*

BERNARD-PAUL HEROUX

All the world's a stage,
And all the men and women merely players:
They have their exits and their entrances;
And one man in his time plays many parts.

WILLIAM SHAKESPEARE

*The Morris is something more than a severe,
cold, unemotional dance, even if it cannot
justly be called a merry, exuberant one.
The movements, though forceful, masculine
and strong, must nevertheless be easily
and gracefully executed, with restraint, too,
and dignity, and even solemnity at times.*

CECIL SHARP

This City now doth
like a garment wear
The beauty of the
morning; silent, bare,
Ships, towers, domes,
theatres, and temples lie
Open unto the fields,
and to the sky;
All bright and glittering
in the smokeless air.

WILLIAM WORDSWORTH

That monarch of the road,
Observer of the Highway Code,
That big six-wheeler
Scarlet-painted
London Transport
Diesel-engined
Ninety-seven horse power
Omnibus!

MICHAEL FLANDERS AND DONALD SWANN

p42~43 Trafalgar Square, London
p44~45 Notting Hill, London
p46 London bus

TRADITIONAL

FISH

CHIPS

ONES
ONS
S ING

Above rose the Coniston Fells in their own shape and colour — not Man's hills but all for themselves the sky and the clouds and a few wild creatures.

DOROTHY WORDSWORTH

67

73

p74 phone box
p75 post box, Gelnridding, Cumbria

The band of silver paleness along the east horizon made even the distant parts of the Great Plain appear dark and near; and the whole enormous landscape bore that impress of reserve, taciturnity, and hesitation which is usual just before the day. The eastward pillars and their architraves stood up blackly against the light.

THOMAS HARDY

p77 Stonehege, Wiltshire

p78 Royal Stuart Tartan Sporran, Edinburgh
p79 Scottish dancing, Royal Braemar Games
p80~81 Black Rock Cottage, Glen Coe

93

Kent, sir — everybody knows Kent —
apples, cherries, hops and women.

CHARLES DICKENS

106

Gazetteer

Angel of the North (pp14-15)
Durham Road, Low Eighton, Gateshead NE9 6AA
T: 01914 784222
W: www.gateshead.gov.uk
Designed by Antony Gormley for Gateshead Council. It weighs
200 tonnes, is 20 metres high and has a 54-metre wing span.

Buckingham Palace (pp18-19)
London SW1A 1AA
T: 020 7766 7300
W: www.royalcollection.org.uk
Buckingham Palace is the official London residence of The
Queen and serves as both a home and office. Its 19 State
Rooms form the heart of the palace and are lavishly furnished
with some of the finest treasures from the Royal Collection.

Caernarforn Castle (pp8-9)
Castle Ditch, Caernarfon, Gwynedd LL55 2AY
T: 01286 677617
W: www.cadw.wales.gov.uk
Famous medieval fortress awarded World Heritage Site status.
The location, in 1969, of the investiture of HRH Prince
Charles as Prince of Wales.

Calanais Standing Stones Visitor Centre (pp72-73)
Callanish, Isle of Lewis, Western Isle HS2 9DY
T: 01851 621422
W: www.calanaisvisitorcentre.co.uk
These standing stones are older than Stonehenge and are one
of the most remote and ancient monuments in Europe. There is
also a visitor centre with multi-lingual interpretation.

Durham Cathedral (pp68-69)
Durham DH1 3EH
T: 01913 864266
W: www.durhamcathedral.co.uk
Durham Cathedral is thought by many to be the finest example
of Norman church architecture in England. It houses the tombs
of St. Cuthbert and The Venerable Bede.

Eden Project (pp28-29)
Bodelva, St Austell, Cornwall PL24 2SG
T: 01726 811911
W: www.edenproject.com
An unforgettable experience in a breathtaking, epic location.
Eden Project is a gateway into the fascinating world of plants
and people.

Edinburgh Castle (pp24-25)
Castle Hill, Edinburgh EH1 2NG
T: 0131 225 9846
Dominating Scotland's capital, parts of this famous castle date
from the Norman period. Mons Meg, the enormous 500-year-
old siege cannon, is located here.

Hadrian's Wall (pp102-103)
Hadrian's Wall, Hexham, Northumberland
T: 01912 691600
W: www.nationaltrail.co.uk/hadrianswall
A 135-kilometre path, providing access to Hadrian's Wall,
opened to the public on 23 May 2003.

Hampton Court Palace (pp38-39)
East Molesey, Surry KT8 9AY
T: 0870 752 7777
W: www.hrp.org.uk
This magnificent palace set in delightful gardens was one of
Henry VIII's favourite palaces. Explore his State Apartments
and those of William III where history is brought to life with
costumed guides.

King's College Chapel (pp26-27)
King's College, Cambridge, Cambridgeshire CB2 1ST
T: 01223 331212
W: www.kings.cam.ac.uk/chapel/
The chapel, founded by Henry VI includes the breathtaking
fan-vault ceiling, stained-glass windows, a carved-oak screen
and Ruben's masterpiece, The Adoration of the Magi.

Shakespeare's Globe (pp30-31)
21 new Globe Walk, Bankside, London SE1 9DT
T: 020 7902 1400
W: www.shakespearesglobe.org
A faithful recreation of the open-air playhouse designed in
1599, where Shakespeare worked and for which he wrote
many of his greatest plays. The theatre season runs from May
to October, with productions of the work of Shakespeare, his
contemporaries and modern authors.

Stonehenge (pp76-77)
Amesbury, Salisbury, Wiltshire SP4 7DE
T: 0870 333 1181
W: www.english-heritage.org.uk
World-famous prehistoric monument built as a ceremonial
centre. Started 5000 years ago and remodelled several times
during the following 1500 years.

Stourhead House and Garden (pp104-105)
Stourton, Warminster, Wiltshire BA12 6QD
T: 01747 841152
W: www.nationaltrust.org.uk
Beautiful landscaped gardens laid out between 1741-80, with lakes, temples, rare trees and plants. The House, begun circa 1721 by Colen Campbell, contains fine paintings and Chippendale furniture.

Telford and Ironbridge Gorge (pp12-13)
Darby House, Lawn Central, Telford,
Shropshire TF3 4BL
T: 01902 202976
W: www.visitironbridge.co.uk
The World Heritage site of Ironbridge Gorge in proximity to stately homes, ancient roman ruins, abbeys, churches and beautiful parks and gardens.

The London Eye (pp92-93)
British Airways London Eye, Riverside Building,
County Hall, Westminster Bridge Road,
London SE1 7PB
T: 0870 990 8883
W: www.londoneye.com
The British Airways London Eye is also known as the Millennium Wheel. It was opened in 1999 and is the largest observation wheel in the world.

The Royal Albert Hall (pp112-113)
Kensington Gore, London SW7 2AP
T: 020 7589 8212
W: www.royalalberthall.com
The Royal Albert Hall is an arts venue dedicated to Queen Victoria's husband and consort, Prince Albert. It was built in 1871 and is home to the Royal Philharmonic Orchestra.

Tower Bridge Exhibition (pp10-11)
Tower Bridge, London SE1 2UP
T: 020 7403 3761
W: www.towerbridge.org.uk
High level walkways located 43 metres above the River Thames — with stunning panoramic views across London — and Victorian Engine Rooms.

York Minster (pp82-83)
Deangate, York, North Yorkshire YO1 7HH
T: 01904 557216
W: www.yorkminster.org
York Minster is the largest medieval Gothic cathedral in northern Europe and a treasure house of 800 years of stained glass.

Image Acknowledgements

Angel, David	8, 66
Bosworth, Daniel	92, 108
Brent, Martin	14, 20, 82, 100, 110
Britainonview.com	4, 31, 32, 36, 54, 56, 72, 76, 78, 80, 99, 104
BTA / Lichfield, Patrick	79
Cornish, Joe	70, 98
De Witt	55
Eden Project	28
Edwards, Rod	26, 58, 75, 88, 96, 102
Guy, VK / Guy, Paul	68
Knight, Martin	84
Libera, Pawel	12, 18, 24, 38, 46, 52
Martin, John	34
McCormick-McAdam	10, 40, 50
Miller, John	60
Porter, Dave	64
Pritchard, Grant	42, 87, 90
Rasmussen, Ingrid	22, 62, 63, 106, 107
Roques-Rogery, Olivier	86
Sellman, David	74
Spaull, Jon	44
Taylor, Howard	95
Teer, Jasmine	112
TNT Magazine	48

All the photographs featured in Heritage Britain are supplied by britainonview.com, the official online image library of VisitBritain.

Britainonview

Quotation Acknowledgements

13   Thomas Telford (1757-1834), Thomas Telford, Anthony Burton, Aurum Press (March 2000)

23   Bernard-Paul Heroux (1900s), source unconfirmed

30   William Shakespeare (1564-1616), As you Like It (1599) act 2, sc. 7, 1.139

25   Cecil Sharp (1859-1924), The Morris Book by Cecil J. Sharp and Herbert C. Macilwaine (Part 1)
        2nd Edition, Novello and Company, London, 1912

41   William Wordsworth (1770-1850), 'Composed upon Westminster Bridge' (1807)

47   Michael Flanders (1922-1975) and Donald Swann (1923-1994), A Transport of Delight (The Omnibus),
        Words by Michael Flanders & Music by Donald Swann © Flanders and Swann. All rights administered by
        Warner/Chapell Music Ltd, London W6 8BS. Reproduced by permission

65   Dorothy Wordsworth (1771-1855), Journals of Dorothy Wordsworth: The Alfoxden Journal 1798, The
        Grasmere Journals 1800-1803, ed. Mary Moorman (New York: Oxford UP, 1971)

76   Thomas Hardy (1840-1928), Tess of the d'Urbervilles, Chapter LVIII, Bantam Classics (1 May, 1984)

P4   Charles Dickens (1812-1870), The Pickwick Papers, Penguin Classic (1 August, 2000)

Particular thanks goes to Mikki Francis of Warner/Chappell Music Ltd

Every attempt has been made to contact current copyright holders of quoted material. Any errors
or omissions will be rectified in future editions or reprints.